This delightful book is the latest in the series of Ladybird books that have been specially planned to help grown-ups with the world about them.

As in the other books in this series, the large clear script, the careful choice of words, the frequent repetition and the thoughtful matching of text with pictures all enable grown-ups to think they have taught themselves to cope. The subject of the book will greatly appeal to grown-ups.

Series 999

THE LADYBIRD
BOOKS FOR GROWN-UPS SERIES

THE
SHED

by

J. A. HAZELEY, N.S.F.W. and J. P. MORRIS, O.M.G.

(Authors of 'Teach Your Dog Darts')

Publishers: Ladybird Books Ltd, Loughborough
Printed in England. If wet, Italy.

The shed is the man's natural hiding-place. It is just like the pub, except nearer to home.

In a minute, Les will throw his children out of his shed and get on with some proper work.

Then, when the coast is clear, he will go to the pub.

Some animals have evolved to carry their shed with them.

This tortoise will withdraw into its shed if threatened by a predator with a request to help peel the potatoes.

In the winter, tortoises conserve energy by spending extended periods in their shed, fast asleep.

Just like humans.

Michael and Gwen are looking for the placemats Gwen's mother bought them for Christmas.

"Quick," says Gwen. "She will be here in twenty minutes!"

"I bet we hid them in here," says Michael, closing himself inside the quiet shed.

Michael says he will not give up looking for the mats in the shed, even if it takes him all day.

Men have built sheds in the most inhospitable environments on the planet.

These men have built their shed near the South Pole.

If anyone wants the men to come back in and run the Hoover round the front room, they have to give six months' notice.

This Antarctic shed is a great place to get things done.

Using your shed as an office is called shedworking.

Bunny works from his shed. He is a freelance cow-whisperer.

At least, that's what he tells his wife. Bunny is unemployed.

A shed is the perfect place to store things that are not quite useful enough to be in your house, but almost useful enough not to be in your bin.

Some of the things in your shed may even turn into heirlooms for your children.

Who knows – in the future there might be a National Museum of Old Phone Chargers. They will pay handsomely for your collection.

Here in Canada, Cliff has built a shed with its own moat.

Cliff's friends use the logs when they come to help with his 00-gauge railway layout. They sometimes bring sandwiches from his wife.

Cliff's wife thinks all marriages should have a moat.

A man needs a private place to do things with his hands.

What would you do with your hands, if you were alone in a shed?

Wallace has taught himself taxidermy. There are so many dead animals full of sawdust in his shed that the door will not shut.

Wallace needs a new shed.

The sheds of the Pharaoh Amenhotep were amongst the most spectacular structures in the Ancient World.

This mighty Pharaoh was buried in 1521 BC in his shed at Kom al-Ahmar, alongside everything he would need in the afterlife: a bundle of rusty sickles, a woven rush box of back issues of *Nile Life*, half a chariot axle assembly and a sacred tin of magnolia satin paint.

A shed is a good place to fix, build and make things.

Omar has made himself a special wooden friend.

Omar's wife cried when she found the plans for this in his shed.

"You won't cry, will you?" says Omar, staring into his friend's painted eyes.

Warren has spent the weekend in his shed. He said he was sanding down some drawers to make them run more smoothly.

Warren's robot has been made from old lawnmower parts. It can walk, talk and hold the door shut.

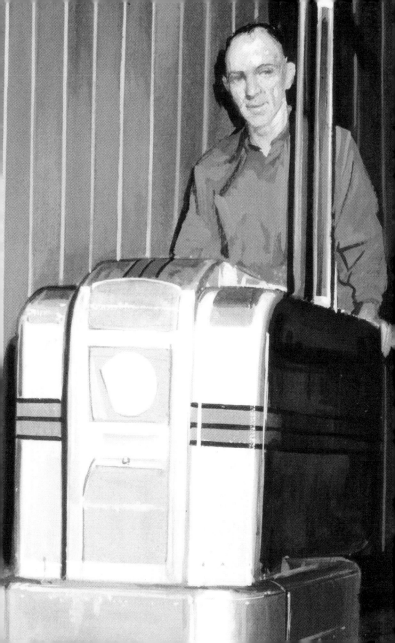

Roland is spending Easter in the shed, sorting his screws.

While his wife and children visit his mother, Roland is separating his screws into flathead, Phillips, PoziDriv, countersunk, double countersunk, bugle head, round head, clutch head, button head, pan head, hex head, flange head, fillister head and miscellaneous. There are also boxes for washers, hooks, pins and a bag for fluff.

"It needed doing," says Roland.

This dream shed belongs to the pop singer Rod Stewart. It has a television, a library of pop magazines and a bath shaped like the charts (with the hot tap in the number one spot).

It is the perfect place to throw a swinging party, but is also a working shed for Rod to do his fretwork, or hide from his wives.

Like many men, Justin uses his shed for home brewing. This year, he has made mild, light ale, continental lager, supermilk, tomato wine, parsnip gin and a fortified onion Lambrini.

This batch of home-brewed Marmite is stronger than the one in the shops, so there must be a policeman present at all times.

Not many people have seen inside this shed. It is the Government Research Shed, half a mile underground at Porton Down.

This high-tech facility is kept ready for use at a moment's notice.

It is where the government will potter in the event of a nuclear attack.

Sheds were important to primitive man, since they provided much needed shelter from primitive family life.

This rudimentary shed is made from sabre-toothed rabbit pelts, mud pies and sticks.

After a meal of mammoth and roots, men would hide here until all the flints were washed up.

Oliver has many important jobs to do around the house, and he needs somewhere quiet to do them.

In his shed, using a quarter-inch squirrel-hair brush, Oliver carefully Tipp-Exes out the designs on the dinner service he inherited from his late wife's mother.

"Filigree is the Devil's work," says Oliver. "Purity is strength."

Some sheds are quite beautiful.

"Come out, Frank," says his wife Margaret.

"I honestly don't know what he gets up to in there," she tells her sister.

If the shed at the end of the garden does not feel far away enough, you can get a second garden, called an allotment.

Cyril has a shed on his allotment, nine miles from his home.

He also has an emergency shed in Italy, for when his wife finds this shed.

The shed is a good place for keeping all the things you need to do odd jobs around the house.

Laurie always has lots of odd jobs to do.

For instance, today he is painting his shed again.

It is the first day of Polly and Toby's school holidays.

For six whole weeks, they will be in the house every day, all day.

Their dad Keith has thought of something they can do together.

"Help me fill the shed with food," says Keith. "And then get out."

In May 1956, Eric Webb of Dagenham emerged from his shed, where he had been pottering since 1938.

He had been reported missing, presumed dead, in 1941 when his house was destroyed by a German incendiary device.

Eric did not know that there had been a war. He immediately returned to his shed and started work rebuilding his home.

It took Tom six years to get planning permission for his garage extension.

Tom's neighbours said the structure would overlook their gardens and block sunlight.

Tom is sure they will change their minds when they see his flying boat.

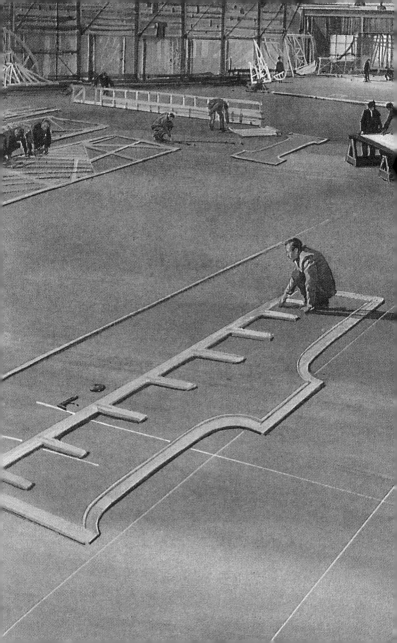

This is the explorer Robert Falcon Scott in the most famous shed of all time.

Scott's second expedition to the Antarctic was a disaster, but his shed was a triumph.

"I'm going outside; I may be some time" are inspirational words that men quote to this day, as they unbolt the back door and vanish down the garden path.

The authors would like to thank the illustrators whose work they have so mercilessly ribbed, and whose glorious craftsmanship was the set-dressing of their childhoods. The inspiration they sparked has never faded.

MICHAEL JOSEPH

UK | USA | Canada | Ireland | Australia
India | New Zealand | South Africa

Michael Joseph is part of the Penguin Random House group of companies whose addresses can be found at global.penguinrandomhouse.com

First published 2015
006

Printed in Italy by L.E.G.O. S.p.A

A CIP catalogue record for this book is available from the British Library

ISBN: 978–0–718–18358–5

www.greenpenguin.co.uk

Penguin Random House is committed to a sustainable future for our business, our readers and our planet. This book is made from Forest Stewardship Council® certified paper.